D1280707

New International Version

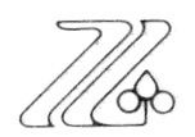

Proverbs and Ecclesiastes

FROM THE New International Version

ZONDERVAN BIBLE PUBLISHERS
OF THE ZONDERVAN CORPORATION
GRAND RAPIDS, MICHIGAN 49506

Proverbs and Ecclesiastes From the New International Version

Published by The Zondervan Corporation
Grand Rapids, Michigan 49506 U.S.A.
Printed in the United States of America

Third printing — 15,000 copies in print

Z-4-78

Also available in the New International Version:
- various editions of the New Testament
- Daniel
- Isaiah

Preface

THIS preliminary translation of Proverbs and Ecclesiastes is part of the New International Version of The Holy Bible. In 1973 the NIV New Testament appeared. Since then, work has been continuing on the Old Testament, which is scheduled for publication in 1978.

The New International Version is neither a paraphrase nor a revision of any previous translation, but a new translation made directly from the original languages. In the Old Testament the Masoretic Text (the traditional Hebrew text) has been generally followed, except where the Dead Sea Scrolls, the Septuagint and other ancient versions, variant manuscript readings and internal evidence have led to corrections in the Masoretic Text.

A transdenominational effort, the New International Version involves over a hundred Biblical scholars from the English-speaking world. All of them are committed to the belief that the Bible is the inspired Word of God. Their aim is to make a translation that is clear and idiomatic, contemporary but not quickly dated, dignified but not stilted. They are therefore seeking simplicity of expression together with sensitive regard for the connotation and sound of the words chosen. Literary stylists work with them in pursuit of this aim.

Where there is uncertainty about the wording of the original text or its precise meaning, footnotes call attention to this. Although sectional headings are inserted in the translation to facilitate reference, they are not an official part of the text. In the translation itself, brackets are occasionally used to indicate words or phrases supplied for clarification.

PREFACE

The Committee on Bible Translation expresses its gratitude to the New York International Bible Society for underwriting the heavy cost of producing the New International Version. The Committee welcomes suggestions and criticisms, which may be sent to the New York International Bible Society at 5 East 48th Street, New York, New York 10017.

Upon request the Society will forward a list of translators and literary consultants associated with the project.

To the praise and glory of God we now offer this portion of the Old Testament of the New International Version.

The Committee on Bible Translation

Proverbs

Proverbs

Prologue: Purpose and Theme

1 The proverbs of Solomon son of David, king of Israel:

[2]for attaining wisdom and discipline;
for understanding words of insight;
[3]for acquiring a disciplined and prudent life,
doing what is right and just and fair;
[4]for giving prudence to the simple,
knowledge and discretion to the young—
[5]let the wise listen and add to their learning,
and let the discerning receive guidance—
[6]for understanding proverbs and parables,
the sayings and riddles of the wise.

[7]The fear of the LORD is the beginning of knowledge,
but fools[a] despise wisdom and discipline.

Exhortations to Embrace Wisdom

Warning Against Enticement

[8]Listen, my son, to your father's instruction
and do not forsake your mother's teaching.
[9]They will be a garland to grace your head
and a chain to adorn your neck.

[a] 7 The Hebrew words rendered *fool* in Proverbs, and often elsewhere in the Old Testament, denote one who is morally deficient.

[10]My son, if sinners entice you,
do not give in to them.
[11]If they say, "Come along with us;
let's lie in wait for someone's blood,
let's waylay some harmless soul;
[12]let's swallow them alive, like the grave,[a]
and whole, like those who go down to the pit;
[13]we will get all sorts of valuable things
and fill our houses with plunder;
[14]throw in your lot with us,
and we will share a common purse"—
[15]my son, do not go along with them,
do not set foot on their paths;
[16]for their feet rush into sin,
they are swift to shed blood.
[17]How useless to spread a net
in full view of all the birds!
[18]These men lie in wait for their own blood;
they waylay only themselves!
[19]Such is the end of all who go after ill-gotten gain;
it takes away the lives of those who get it.

Warning Against Rejecting Wisdom

[20]Wisdom calls aloud in the street,
she raises her voice in the public squares;
[21]at the head of the noisy streets[b] she cries out,
in the gateways of the city she makes her speech:

[22]"How long will you simple ones[c] love your simple ways?
How long will mockers delight in mockery
and fools hate knowledge?

[a] *12* Hebrew *Sheol*   [b] *21* Hebrew; Septuagint *on the tops of the walls*
[c] *22* The Hebrew word rendered *simple* in Proverbs generally denotes one without moral direction and inclined to evil.

[23]If you had responded to my rebuke,
I would have poured out my heart to you
and made my thoughts known to you.
[24]But since you rejected me when I called
and no one gave heed when I stretched out my hand,
[25]since you ignored all my advice
and would not accept my rebuke,
[26]I in turn will laugh at your disaster;
I will mock when calamity overtakes you—
[27]when calamity overtakes you like a storm,
when disaster sweeps over you like a whirlwind,
when distress and troubles overwhelm you.

[28]"Then they will call to me but I will not answer;
they will look for me but will not find me.
[29]Since they hated knowledge
and did not choose to fear the LORD,
[30]since they would not accept my advice
and spurned my rebuke,
[31]they will eat the fruit of their ways
and be filled with the fruit of their schemes.
[32]For the waywardness of the simple will kill them,
and the complacency of fools will destroy them;
[33]but whoever listens to me will live in safety
and be at ease, without fear of harm."

Moral Benefits of Wisdom

2 My son, if you accept my words
and store up my commands within you,
[2]turning your ear to wisdom
and applying your heart to understanding,
[3]and if you call out for insight
and cry aloud for understanding,

[4]and if you look for it as for silver
and search for it as for hidden treasure,
[5]then you will understand the fear of the LORD
and find the knowledge of God.
[6]For the LORD gives wisdom,
and from his mouth come knowledge and understanding.
[7]He holds victory in store for the upright,
he is a shield to those whose walk is blameless,
[8]for he guards the course of the just
and protects the way of his faithful ones.

[9]Then you will understand what is right and just
and fair—every good path.
[10]For wisdom will enter your heart,
and knowledge will be pleasant to your soul.
[11]Discretion will protect you,
and understanding will guard you.

[12]Wisdom will save you from the ways of wicked men,
from men whose words are perverse,
[13]who leave the straight paths
to walk in dark ways,
[14]who delight in doing wrong
and rejoice in the perverseness of evil,
[15]whose paths are crooked
and who are devious in their ways.

[16]It will save you also from the adulteress,
from the wayward wife with her seductive words,
[17]who has left the partner of her youth
and ignored the covenant she made before God.[a]
[18]For her house leads down to death

[a] *17* Or *covenant of her God*

and her paths to the spirits of the dead.
[19]None who go to her return
or attain the paths of life.

[20]Thus you will walk in the ways of good men
and keep to the paths of the righteous.
[21]For the upright will live in the land,
and the blameless will remain in it;
[22]but the wicked will be cut off from the land,
and the unfaithful will be torn from it.

Further Benefits of Wisdom

3 My son, do not forget my teaching,
but keep my commands in your heart,
[2]for they will prolong your life many years
and bring you prosperity.

[3]Let love and faithfulness never leave you;
bind them around your neck,
write them on the tablet of your heart.
[4]Then you will win favor and a good name
in the sight of God and man.

[5]Trust in the LORD with all your heart
and lean not on your own understanding;
[6]in all your ways acknowledge him,
and he will make your paths straight.

[7]Do not be wise in your own eyes;
fear the LORD and shun evil.
[8]This will bring health to your body
and nourishment to your bones.

[9]Honor the LORD with your wealth,
with the firstfruits of all your produce;
[10]then your barns will be filled to overflowing,
and your vats will brim over with new wine.

[11]My son, do not despise the LORD's discipline
and do not resent his rebuke,
[12]because the LORD disciplines those he loves,
as a father[a] the son he delights in.

[13]Blessed is the man who finds wisdom,
the man who gains understanding,
[14]for she is more profitable than silver
and yields better returns than gold.
[15]She is more precious than rubies;
nothing you desire can compare with her.
[16]Long life is in her right hand;
in her left hand are riches and honor.
[17]Her ways are pleasant ways,
and all her paths are peace.
[18]She is a tree of life to those who embrace her;
those who lay hold of her will be blessed.

[19]By wisdom the LORD laid the earth's foundations,
by understanding he set the heavens in place;
[20]by his knowledge the deeps were divided,
and the clouds let drop the dew.

[21]My son, preserve sound judgment and
discernment,
do not let them out of your sight;
[22]they will be life for you,
an ornament to grace your neck.
[23]Then you will go on your way in safety,
and your foot will not stumble;
[24]when you lie down, you will not be afraid;
when you lie down, your sleep will be sweet.
[25]Have no fear of sudden disaster
or of the ruin that overtakes the wicked,
[26]for the LORD will be your confidence

[a] *12* Hebrew; Septuagint *and he punishes*

and will keep your foot from being snared.

[27]Do not withhold good from those who deserve it,
when it is in your power to act.
[28]Do not say to your neighbor,
"Come back later; I'll give it tomorrow"—
when you now have it with you.

[29]Do not plot harm against your neighbor,
who lives trustfully near you.
[30]Do not accuse a man for no reason—
when he has done you no harm.

[31]Do not envy a violent man
or choose any of his ways,
[32]for the LORD detests a perverse man
but takes the upright into his confidence.

[33]The LORD's curse is on the house of the wicked,
but he blesses the home of the righteous.
[34]He mocks proud mockers
but gives grace to the humble.
[35]The wise inherit honor,
but fools he holds up to shame.

Wisdom Is Supreme

4 Listen, my sons, to a father's instruction;
pay attention and gain understanding.
[2]I give you sound learning,
so do not forsake my teaching.
[3]When I was a boy in my father's house,
still tender, and an only child of my mother,
[4]he taught me and said,
"Lay hold of my words with all your heart;
keep my commands and you will live.
[5]Get wisdom, get understanding;
do not forget my words or swerve from them.

[6]Do not forsake wisdom, and she will protect you;
love her, and she will watch over you.
[7]Wisdom is supreme; therefore get wisdom.
Though it cost all you have,[a] get
understanding.
[8]Esteem her, and she will exalt you;
embrace her, and she will honor you.
[9]She will set a garland of grace on your head
and present you with a crown of splendor."

[10]Listen, my son, accept what I say,
and the years of your life will be many.
[11]I guide you in the way of wisdom
and lead you along straight paths.
[12]When you walk, your steps will not be
hampered;
when you run, you will not stumble.
[13]Hold on to instruction, do not let it go;
guard it well, for it is your life.
[14]Do not set foot on the path of the wicked
or walk in the way of evil men.
[15]Avoid it, do not travel on it;
turn from it and go on your way.
[16]For they cannot sleep till they do evil;
they are robbed of slumber till they make
someone fall.
[17]They eat the bread of wickedness
and drink the wine of violence.

[18]The path of the righteous is like the first gleam
of dawn,
shining ever brighter till the full light of day.
[19]But the way of the wicked is like deep darkness;
they do not know what makes them stumble.

[a] 7 Or *Whatever else you get*

[20]My son, pay attention to what I say;
listen closely to my words.
[21]Do not let them out of your sight,
keep them within your heart;
[22]for they are life to those who find them
and health to a man's whole body.
[23]Above all else, guard your heart,
for it is the wellspring of life.
[24]Put away perversity from your mouth;
keep corrupt talk far from your lips.
[25]Let your eyes look straight ahead,
fix your gaze directly before you.
[26]Make level[a] paths for your feet
and take only ways that are firm.
[27]Do not swerve to the right or the left;
keep your foot from evil.

Warning Against Adultery

5 My son, pay attention to my wisdom,
listen well to my words of insight,
[2]that you may maintain discretion
and your lips may preserve knowledge.
[3]For the lips of an adulteress drip honey,
and her speech is smoother than oil;
[4]but in the end she is bitter as gall,
sharp as a double-edged sword.
[5]Her feet go down to death;
her steps lead straight to the grave.[b]
[6]She gives no thought to the way of life;
her paths are crooked, but she knows it not.

[7]Now then, my sons, listen to me;
do not turn aside from what I say.
[8]Keep to a path far from her,
do not go near the door of her house,

[a] 26 Or *Consider the* [b] 5 Hebrew *Sheol*

[9]lest you give your best strength to others
and your years to one who is cruel,
[10]lest strangers feast on your wealth
and your toil enrich another man's house.
[11]At the end of your life you will groan,
when your flesh and body are spent.
[12]You will say, "How I hated discipline!
How my heart spurned correction!
[13]I would not obey my teachers
or listen to my instructors.
[14]I have come to the brink of utter ruin
in the midst of the whole assembly."

[15]Drink water from your own cistern,
running water from your own well.
[16]Should your springs overflow in the streets,
your streams of water in the public
squares?
[17]Let them be yours alone,
never to be shared with strangers.
[18]May your fountain be blessed,
and may you rejoice in the wife of your
youth.
[19]A loving doe, a graceful deer—
may her breasts satisfy you always,
may you ever be captivated by her love.
[20]Why be captivated, my son, by an adulteress?
Why embrace the bosom of another man's
wife?

[21]For a man's ways are in full view of the LORD,
and he examines all his paths.
[22]The evil deeds of a wicked man ensnare him;
the cords of his sin hold him fast.
[23]He will die for lack of discipline,
led astray by his own great folly.

Warnings Against Folly

6 My son, if you have put up security for your neighbor,
if you have struck hands in pledge for another,
[2]if you have been trapped by what you said,
ensnared by the words of your mouth,
[3]then do this, my son, to free yourself,
since you have fallen into your neighbor's hands:
Go and humble yourself;
press your plea with your neighbor!
[4]Allow no sleep to your eyes,
no slumber to your eyelids.
[5]Free yourself, like a gazelle from the hand of the hunter,
like a bird from the snare of the fowler.

[6]Go to the ant, you sluggard;
consider its ways and be wise!
[7]It has no commander,
no overseer or ruler,
[8]yet it stores its provisions in summer
and gathers its food at harvest.

[9]How long will you lie there, you sluggard?
When will you get up from your sleep?
[10]A little sleep, a little slumber,
a little folding of the hands to rest—
[11]and poverty will come on you like a bandit
and scarcity like an armed man.[a]

[12]A scoundrel and villain,
who goes about with a corrupt mouth,
[13] who winks with his eye,
signals with his feet

[a] 11 Or *like a vagrant / and scarcity like a beggar*

and motions with his fingers,
[14] who plots evil with deceit in his heart—
he always stirs up dissension.
[15]Therefore in an instant disaster will overtake him;
he will suddenly be destroyed—without remedy.

[16]There are six things the LORD hates,
seven that are detestable to him:
[17] haughty eyes,
a lying tongue,
hands that shed innocent blood,
[18] a heart that devises wicked schemes,
feet that are quick to rush into evil,
[19] a false witness who pours out lies
and a man who stirs up dissension among brothers.

Warning Against Adultery

[20]My son, keep your father's commands
and do not forsake your mother's teaching.
[21]Bind them upon your heart forever;
fasten them around your neck.
[22]When you walk, they will guide you;
when you sleep, they will watch over you;
when you awake, they will speak to you.
[23]For these commands are a lamp, this teaching is a light,
and the corrections of discipline are the way to life,
[24]keeping you from the immoral woman,
from the smooth tongue of the wayward wife.
[25]Do not lust in your heart after her beauty
or let her captivate you with her eyes,
[26]for the prostitute reduces you to a loaf of bread,
and the adulteress preys upon your very life.

[27]Can a man scoop fire into his lap
without his clothes being burned?
[28]Can a man walk on hot coals
without his feet being scorched?
[29]So is he who sleeps with another man's wife;
no one who touches her will go unpunished.

[30]Men do not despise a thief if he steals
to satisfy his hunger when he is starving.
[31]Yet if he is caught, he must pay sevenfold,
though it costs him all the wealth of his house.
[32]But a man who commits adultery lacks judgment;
whoever does so destroys himself.
[33]Blows and disgrace are his lot,
and his shame will never be wiped away;
[34]for jealousy arouses a husband's fury,
and he will show no mercy when he takes
revenge.
[35]He will not accept any compensation;
he will refuse the bribe, however great it is.

Warning Against the Adulteress

7 My son, keep my words
and store up my commands within you.
[2]Keep my commands and you will live;
guard my teachings as the apple of your eye.
[3]Bind them on your fingers;
write them on the tablet of your heart.
[4]Say to wisdom, "You are my sister,"
and call understanding your kinsman;
[5]they will keep you from the adulteress,
from the wayward wife with her seductive
words.

[6]At the window of my house
I looked out through the lattice.
[7]I saw among the simple,

I noticed among the young men,
a youth who lacked judgment.
[8]He was going down the street near her corner,
walking along in the direction of her house
[9]at twilight, as the day was fading,
as the dark of night set in.

[10]Then out came a woman to meet him,
dressed like a prostitute and with crafty intent.
[11](She is loud and defiant,
her feet never stay at home;
[12]now in the street, now in the squares,
at every corner she lurks.)
[13]She took hold of him and kissed him
and with a brazen face she said:

[14]"I have peace offerings at home;
today I fulfilled my vows.
[15]So I came out to meet you;
I looked for you and have found you!
[16]I have covered my bed
with colored linens from Egypt.
[17]I have perfumed my bed
with myrrh, aloes and cinnamon.
[18]Come, let's drink deep of love till morning;
let's enjoy ourselves with love!
[19]My husband is not at home;
he has gone on a long journey.
[20]He took his purse filled with money
and will not be home till full moon."

[21]With persuasive words she led him astray;
she seduced him with her smooth talk.
[22]All at once he followed her
like an ox going to the slaughter,
like a deer[a] stepping into a noose[b]

[a] 22 Septuagint and Syriac; Hebrew *fool* [b] 22 The meaning of the Hebrew of this line is uncertain.

[23] till an arrow pierces his liver,
like a bird darting into a snare,
little knowing it will cost him his life.

[24]Now then, my sons, listen to me;
pay attention to what I say.
[25]Do not let your heart turn to her ways
or stray into her paths.
[26]Many are the victims she has brought down;
her slain are a mighty throng.
[27]Her house is a highway to the grave,[a]
leading down to the chambers of death.

Wisdom's Appeal

8 Does not wisdom call out?
Does not understanding raise her voice?
[2]On the heights along the way,
where the paths meet, she takes her stand;
[3]beside the gates leading into the city,
at the entrances, she cries aloud:
[4]"To you, O men, I call out;
I raise my voice to all mankind.
[5]You who are simple, gain prudence;
you who are foolish, gain understanding.
[6]Listen, for I have worthy things to say;
I open my lips to speak what is right.
[7]My mouth speaks what is true,
for my lips detest wickedness.
[8]All the words of my mouth are just;
none of them is crooked or perverse.
[9]To the discerning all of them are right;
they are faultless to those who have
knowledge.
[10]Choose my instruction instead of silver,
knowledge rather than choice gold,

[a] *27* Hebrew *Sheol*

[11]for wisdom is more precious than rubies,
and nothing you desire can compare with her.

[12]"I, wisdom, dwell together with prudence;
I possess knowledge and discretion.
[13]To fear the LORD is to hate evil;
I hate pride and arrogance,
evil behavior and perverse speech.
[14]Counsel and sound judgment are mine;
I have understanding and power.
[15]By me kings reign
and rulers make laws that are just;
[16]by me princes govern,
and all nobles who rule on earth.[a]
[17]I love those who love me,
and those who seek me find me.
[18]With me are riches and honor,
enduring wealth and prosperity.
[19]My fruit is better than fine gold;
what I yield surpasses choice silver.
[20]I walk in the way of righteousness,
along the paths of justice,
[21]bestowing wealth on those who love me
and making their treasuries full.

[22]"The LORD possessed me[b] at the beginning of his work,[c]
before his deeds of old;
[23]I was appointed[d] from eternity,
from the beginning, before the world began.
[24]When there were no oceans, I was given birth,
when there were no springs abounding with water;
[25]before the mountains were settled in place,

[a] *16* Many Hebrew manuscripts and Septuagint; other Hebrew manuscripts *all righteous rulers* [b] *22* Or *The LORD brought me forth* [c] *22* Or *way;* or *dominion*
[d] *23* Or *fashioned*

before the hills, I was given birth,
[26]before he made the earth or its fields
or any of the dust of the world.
[27]I was there when he set the heavens in place,
when he marked out the horizon on the face of the deep,
[28]when he established the clouds above
and fixed securely the fountains of the deep,
[29]when he gave the sea its boundary
so the waters would not overstep his command,
and when he marked out the foundations of the earth.
[30] Then I was the craftsman at his side.
I was filled with delight day after day,
rejoicing always in his presence,
[31]rejoicing in his whole world
and delighting in mankind.

[32]"Now then, my sons, listen to me;
blessed are those who keep my ways.
[33]Listen to my instruction and be wise;
do not ignore it.
[34]Blessed is the man who listens to me,
watching daily at my doors,
waiting at my doorway.
[35]For whoever finds me finds life
and receives favor from the LORD.
[36]But whoever fails to find me harms himself;
all who hate me love death."

Invitations of Wisdom and of Folly

9 Wisdom has built her house;
she has hewn out its seven pillars.
[2]She has prepared her meat and mixed her wine;
she has also set her table.

[3]She has sent out her maids, and she calls
from the highest point of the city:
[4]"Let all who are simple come in here!"
she says to those who lack judgment.
[5]"Come, eat my food
and drink the wine I have mixed.
[6]Leave your simple ways and you will live;
walk in the way of understanding.

[7]"Whoever corrects a mocker brings on insult;
whoever rebukes a wicked man incurs abuse.
[8]Do not rebuke a mocker or he will hate you;
rebuke a wise man and he will love you.
[9]Instruct a wise man and he will be wiser still;
teach a righteous man and he will add to his learning.

[10]"The fear of the LORD is the beginning of wisdom,
and knowledge of the Holy One is understanding.
[11]For through me your days will be many,
and years will be added to your life.
[12]If you are wise, your wisdom will reward you;
if you are a mocker, you alone will suffer."

[13]The woman Folly is loud;
she is undisciplined and without knowledge.
[14]She sits at the door of her house,
on a seat at the highest point of the city,
[15]calling out to those who pass by,
who go straight on their way:
[16]"Let all who are simple come in here!"
she says to those who lack judgment.
[17]"Stolen water is sweet;
food eaten in secret is delicious!"

[18]But little do they know that the dead are there,
that her guests are in the depths of the grave.[a]

Proverbs of Solomon

10 The proverbs of Solomon:

A wise son brings joy to his father,
but a foolish son grief to his mother.

[2]Ill-gotten treasures are of no value,
but righteousness delivers from death.

[3]The LORD does not let the righteous go hungry
but he thwarts the craving of the wicked.

[4]Lazy hands make a man poor,
but diligent hands bring wealth.

[5]He who gathers crops in summer is a wise son,
but he who sleeps during harvest is a disgraceful son.

[6]Blessings crown the head of the righteous,
but violence overwhelms the mouth of the wicked.[b]

[7]The memory of the righteous will be a blessing,
but the name of the wicked will rot.

[8]The wise in heart accept commands,
but a chattering fool comes to ruin.

[9]The man of integrity walks securely,
but he who takes crooked paths will be found out.

[10]He who winks maliciously causes grief,
and a chattering fool comes to ruin.

[11]The mouth of the righteous is a fountain of life,

[a] *18* Hebrew *Sheol* [b] *6* Or *but the mouth of the wicked conceals violence*

but violence overwhelms the mouth of the wicked.[a]

[12]Hatred stirs up dissension,
but love covers over all wrongs.

[13]Wisdom is found on the lips of the discerning,
but a rod is for the back of him who lacks judgment.

[14]Wise men store up knowledge,
but the mouth of a fool invites ruin.

[15]The wealth of the rich is their fortified city,
but poverty is the ruin of the poor.

[16]The wages of the righteous bring them life
but the income of the wicked brings them punishment.

[17]He who heeds discipline shows the way to life,
but whoever ignores correction leads others astray.

[18]He who conceals his hatred has lying lips,
and whoever spreads slander is a fool.

[19]When words are many, sin is not absent,
but he who holds his tongue is wise.

[20]The tongue of the righteous is choice silver,
but the heart of the wicked is of little value.

[21]The lips of the righteous nourish many,
but fools die for lack of judgment.

[22]The blessing of the LORD brings wealth,
and he adds no trouble to it.

[23]A fool finds pleasure in evil conduct,
but a man of understanding delights in wisdom.

[a] *11* Or *but the mouth of the wicked conceals violence*

[24]What the wicked dreads will overtake him;
what the righteous desire will be granted.

[25]When the storm has swept by, the wicked are gone,
but the righteous stand firm forever.

[26]As vinegar to the teeth and smoke to the eyes,
so is a sluggard to those who send him.

[27]The fear of the LORD adds length to life,
but the years of the wicked are cut short.

[28]The prospect of the righteous is joy,
but the hopes of the wicked come to nothing.

[29]The way of the LORD is a refuge for the righteous,
but it is the ruin of those who do evil.

[30]The righteous will never be uprooted,
but the wicked will not remain in the land.

[31]The mouth of the righteous brings forth wisdom,
but a perverse tongue will be cut out.

[32]The lips of the righteous know what is fitting,
but the mouth of the wicked only what is perverse.

11

The LORD abhors dishonest scales,
but accurate weights are his delight.

[2]When pride comes, then comes disgrace,
but with humility comes wisdom.

[3]The integrity of the upright guides them,
but the unfaithful are destroyed by their duplicity.

[4]Wealth is worthless in the day of wrath,
but righteousness delivers from death.

[5]The righteousness of the blameless makes a
straight way for them,
but the wicked are brought down by their
own wickedness.

[6]The righteousness of the upright delivers them,
but the unfaithful are trapped by evil desires.

[7]When a wicked man dies, his hope perishes;
all he expected from his power comes to
nothing.

[8]The righteous man is rescued from trouble,
and it comes on the wicked instead.

[9]With his mouth the godless destroys his
neighbor,
but through knowledge the righteous escape.

[10]When the righteous prosper, the city rejoices;
when the wicked perish, there are shouts of
joy.

[11]Through the blessing of the upright a city is
exalted,
but by the mouth of the wicked it is
destroyed.

[12]A man who lacks judgment derides his neighbor,
but a man of understanding holds his tongue.

[13]A gossip betrays a confidence,
but a trustworthy man keeps a secret.

[14]For lack of guidance a nation falls,
but many advisers make victory sure.

[15]He who puts up security for another will surely
suffer,
but whoever refuses to strike hands in pledge
is safe.

[16]A kind-hearted woman gains respect,
but ruthless men gain only wealth.

[17]A kind man benefits himself,
but a cruel man brings himself harm.

[18]The wicked man earns deceptive wages,
but he who sows righteousness reaps a sure
reward.

[19]The truly righteous man attains life,
but he who pursues evil goes to his death.

[20]The LORD detests men of perverse heart
but he delights in those whose ways are
blameless.

[21]Be sure of this: The wicked will not go
unpunished,
but those who are righteous will go free.

[22]Like a gold ring in a pig's snout
is a beautiful woman who shows no discretion.

[23]The desire of the righteous ends only in good,
but the hope of the wicked only in wrath.

[24]One man gives freely, yet gains even more;
another withholds unduly, but comes to
poverty.

[25]A generous man will prosper;
he who refreshes others will himself be
refreshed.

[26]People curse the man who hoards grain,
but blessing crowns him who is willing to
sell.

[27]He who seeks good finds good will,
but evil comes to him who searches for it.

[28]Whoever trusts in his riches will fall,
but the righteous will thrive like a green leaf.

[29]He who brings trouble on his family will inherit only wind,
and the fool will be servant to the wise.

[30]The fruit of the righteous is a tree of life,
and he who wins souls is wise.

[31]If the righteous receive their due on earth,
how much more the ungodly and the sinner!

12 Whoever loves discipline loves knowledge,
but he who hates correction is stupid.

[2]A good man obtains favor from the LORD,
but the LORD condemns a crafty man.

[3]A man cannot be established through wickedness,
but the righteous cannot be uprooted.

[4]A wife of noble character is her husband's crown,
but a disgraceful wife is like decay in his bones.

[5]The plans of the righteous are just,
but the advice of the wicked is deceitful.

[6]The words of the wicked lie in wait for blood,
but the speech of the upright rescues them.

[7]Wicked men are overthrown and are no more,
but the house of the righteous stands firm.

[8]A man is praised according to his wisdom,
but men with warped minds are despised.

[9]Better to be a nobody and yet have a servant

than pretend to be somebody and have no
food.

[10]A righteous man cares for the needs of his
animal,
but the kindest acts of the wicked are cruel.

[11]He who works his land will have abundant food,
but he who chases fantasies lacks judgment.

[12]The wicked desire the plunder of evil men,
but the root of the righteous flourishes.

[13]An evil man is trapped by his sinful talk,
but a righteous man escapes trouble.

[14]From the fruit of his lips a man is filled with
good things
as surely as the work of his hands rewards
him.

[15]The way of a fool seems right to him,
but a wise man listens to advice.

[16]A fool shows his annoyance at once,
but a prudent man overlooks an insult.

[17]A truthful witness gives honest testimony,
but a false witness tells lies.

[18]Reckless words pierce like a sword,
but the tongue of the wise brings healing.

[19]Truthful lips endure forever,
but a lying tongue lasts only a moment.

[20]There is deceit in the hearts of those who plot
evil,
but joy for those who promote peace.

[21]No harm befalls the righteous,
but the wicked have their fill of trouble.

22The LORD detests lying lips,
but he delights in men who are truthful.

23A prudent man keeps his knowledge to himself,
but the heart of fools blurts out folly.

24Diligent hands will rule,
but laziness ends in slave labor.

25An anxious heart weighs a man down,
but a kind word cheers him up.

26A righteous man is cautious in friendship,[a]
but the way of the wicked leads them astray.

27The lazy man does not roast[b] his game,
but the diligent man prizes his possessions.

28In the way of righteousness there is life;
along that path is immortality.

13 A wise son heeds his father's instruction,
but a mocker does not listen to rebuke.

2From the fruit of his lips a man enjoys good things,
but the unfaithful have a craving for violence.

3He who guards his lips guards his soul,
but he who speaks rashly will come to ruin.

4The sluggard craves and gets nothing,
but the desires of the diligent are fully satisfied.

5The righteous hate what is false,
but the wicked bring shame and disgrace.

6Righteousness guards the man of integrity,
but wickedness overthrows the sinner.

[a] 26 Or *man is a guide to his neighbor* [b] 27 The meaning of the Hebrew word is uncertain.

[7]One man pretends to be rich, yet has nothing;
another pretends to be poor, yet has great wealth.

[8]A man's riches may ransom his life,
but a poor man hears no threat.

[9]The light of the righteous shines brightly,
but the lamp of the wicked is snuffed out.

[10]Pride only breeds quarrels,
but wisdom is found in those who take advice.

[11]Dishonest money dwindles away,
but he who gathers money little by little makes it grow.

[12]Hope deferred makes the heart sick,
but a longing fulfilled is a tree of life.

[13]He who scorns instruction will pay for it,
but he who respects a command is rewarded.

[14]The teaching of the wise is a fountain of life,
turning a man from the snares of death.

[15]Good understanding wins favor,
but the way of the unfaithful is hard.[a]

[16]Every prudent man acts out of knowledge,
but a fool exposes his folly.

[17]A wicked messenger falls into trouble,
but a trustworthy envoy brings healing.

[18]He who ignores discipline comes to poverty and shame,
but whoever heeds correction is honored.

[19]A longing fulfilled is sweet to the soul,
but fools detest turning from evil.

[a] 15 Or *unfaithful does not endure*

[20]He who walks with the wise grows wise,
but a companion of fools suffers harm.

[21]Misfortune pursues the sinner,
but prosperity is the reward of the righteous.

[22]A good man leaves an inheritance for his children's children,
but a sinner's wealth is stored up for the righteous.

[23]A poor man's field may produce abundant food,
but injustice sweeps it away.

[24]He who spares the rod hates his son,
but he who loves him is careful to discipline him.

[25]The righteous eat to their hearts' content,
but the stomach of the wicked goes hungry.

14 The wise woman builds her house,
but with her own hands the foolish one tears hers down.

[2]He whose walk is upright fears the LORD,
but he whose ways are devious despises him.

[3]A fool's talk brings a rod to his back,
but the lips of the wise protect them.

[4]Where there are no oxen, the manger is empty,
but from the strength of an ox comes an abundant harvest.

[5]A truthful witness does not deceive,
but a false witness pours out lies.

[6]The mocker seeks wisdom and finds none,
but knowledge comes easily to the discerning.

[7]Stay away from a foolish man,
for you will not find knowledge on his lips.

[8]The wisdom of the prudent is to give thought to
their ways,
but the folly of fools is deception.

[9]Fools mock at making amends for sin,
but good will is found among the upright.

[10]Each heart knows its own bitterness,
and no one else can share its joy.

[11]The house of the wicked will be destroyed,
but the tent of the upright will flourish.

[12]There is a way that seems right to a man,
but in the end it leads to death.

[13]Even in laughter the heart may ache,
and joy may end in grief.

[14]The faithless will be fully repaid for their ways,
and the good man rewarded for his.

[15]A simple man believes anything,
but a prudent man gives thought to his steps.

[16]A wise man fears the LORD and shuns evil,
but a fool is hotheaded and reckless.

[17]A quick-tempered man does foolish things,
and a crafty man is hated.

[18]The simple inherit folly,
but the prudent are crowned with knowledge.

[19]Evil men will bow down in the presence of the
good,
and the wicked at the gates of the righteous.

[20]The poor are shunned even by their neighbors,
but the rich have many friends.

[21]He who despises his neighbor sins,
but blessed is he who is kind to the needy.

[22]Do not those who plot evil go astray?
But those who plan good find[a] love and faithfulness.

[23]All hard work brings a profit,
but mere talk leads only to poverty.

[24]The wealth of the wise is their crown,
but the folly of fools yields folly.

[25]A truthful witness saves lives,
but a false witness is deceitful.

[26]He who fears the LORD has a secure fortress,
and for his children it will be a refuge.

[27]The fear of the LORD is a fountain of life,
turning a man from the snares of death.

[28]A large population is a king's glory,
but without subjects a prince is ruined.

[29]A patient man has great understanding,
but a quick-tempered man displays folly.

[30]A heart at peace gives life to the body,
but envy rots the bones.

[31]He who oppresses the poor shows contempt for their Maker,
but whoever is kind to the needy honors God.

[32]When calamity comes, the wicked are brought down,
but even in death the righteous have a refuge.

[33]Wisdom reposes in the heart of the discerning

[a] 22 Or *show*

and even among fools she lets herself be
known.[a]

[34]Righteousness exalts a nation,
but sin is a disgrace to any people.

[35]A king delights in a wise servant,
but a shameful servant incurs his wrath.

15 A gentle answer turns away wrath,
but a harsh word stirs up anger.

[2]The tongue of the wise commends knowledge,
but the mouth of the fool gushes folly.

[3]The eyes of the LORD are everywhere,
keeping watch on the wicked and the good.

[4]The tongue that brings healing is a tree of life,
but a deceitful tongue crushes the spirit.

[5]A fool spurns his father's discipline,
but whoever heeds correction shows prudence.

[6]The house of the righteous contains great
treasure,
but the income of the wicked brings them
trouble.

[7]The lips of the wise spread knowledge;
not so the hearts of fools.

[8]The LORD detests the sacrifice of the wicked,
but the prayer of the upright pleases him.

[9]The LORD detests the way of the wicked
but he loves those who pursue righteousness.

[10]Stern discipline awaits him who leaves the path;
he who hates correction will die.

[a] 33 Hebrew; Septuagint and Syriac *but in the heart of fools she is not known*

[11]Death and Destruction[a] lie open before the LORD—
how much more the hearts of men!

[12]A mocker resents correction;
he will not consult the wise.

[13]A happy heart makes the face cheerful,
but heartache crushes the spirit.

[14]The discerning heart seeks knowledge,
but the mouth of a fool feeds on folly.

[15]All the days of the oppressed are wretched,
but the cheerful heart has a continual feast.

[16]Better a little with the fear of the LORD
than great wealth with turmoil.

[17]Better a meal of vegetables where there is love
than a fattened calf with hatred.

[18]A hot-tempered man stirs up dissension,
but a patient man calms a quarrel.

[19]The way of the sluggard is blocked with thorns,
but the path of the upright is a highway.

[20]A wise son brings joy to his father,
but a foolish man despises his mother.

[21]Folly delights a man who lacks judgment,
but a man of understanding keeps a straight course.

[22]Plans fail for lack of counsel,
but with many advisers they succeed.

[23]A man finds joy in giving an apt reply—
and how good is a timely word!

[a] *11* Hebrew *Sheol and Abaddon*

[24]The path of life leads upward for the wise
to keep him from going down to the grave.[a]

[25]The LORD tears down the proud man's house
but he keeps the widow's boundaries intact.

[26]The LORD detests the thoughts of the wicked,
but those of the pure are pleasing to him.

[27]A greedy man brings trouble to his family,
but he who hates bribes will live.

[28]The heart of the righteous weighs its answers,
but the mouth of the wicked gushes evil.

[29]The LORD is far from the wicked
but he hears the prayer of the righteous.

[30]A cheerful look brings joy to the heart,
and good news gives health to the bones.

[31]He who listens to a life-giving rebuke
will be at home among the wise.

[32]He who ignores discipline despises himself,
but whoever heeds correction gains
understanding.

[33]The fear of the LORD teaches a man wisdom,[b]
and humility comes before honor.

16 To man belong the plans of the heart,
but from the LORD comes the reply of the
tongue.

[2]All a man's ways seem innocent to him,
but motives are weighed by the LORD.

[3]Commit to the LORD whatever you do,
and your plans will succeed.

[a] 24 Hebrew *Sheol*   [b] 33 Or *Wisdom teaches the fear of the LORD*

[4]The LORD works out everything for his own
ends—
even the wicked for a day of disaster.

[5]The LORD detests all the proud of heart.
Be sure of this: They will not go unpunished.

[6]Through love and faithfulness sin is atoned for;
through the fear of the LORD a man avoids
evil.

[7]When a man's ways are pleasing to the LORD,
he makes even his enemies live at peace with
him.

[8]Better a little with righteousness
than much gain with injustice.

[9]In his heart a man plans his course,
but the LORD determines his steps.

[10]The lips of a king speak as an oracle,
and his mouth should not betray justice.

[11]Honest scales and balances are from the LORD;
all the weights in the bag are of his making.

[12]Kings detest wrongdoing,
for a throne is established through
righteousness.

[13]Kings take pleasure in honest lips;
they value a man who speaks the truth.

[14]A king's wrath is a messenger of death,
but a wise man will appease it.

[15]When a king's face brightens, it means life;
his favor is like a rain cloud in spring.

[16]How much better to get wisdom than gold,
to choose understanding rather than silver!

17The highway of the upright avoids evil;
he who guards his way guards his soul.

18Pride goes before destruction,
a haughty spirit before a fall.

19Better to be lowly in spirit and among the oppressed
than to share plunder with the proud.

20Whoever gives heed to instruction prospers,
and blessed is he who trusts in the LORD.

21The wise in heart are called discerning,
and pleasant words promote instruction.[a]

22Understanding is a fountain of life to those who have it,
but folly brings punishment to fools.

23A wise man's heart guides his mouth,
and his lips promote instruction.[b]

24Pleasant words are a honeycomb,
sweet to the soul and healing to the bones.

25There is a way that seems right to a man
but in the end it leads to death.

26The laborer's appetite works for him;
his hunger drives him on.

27A scoundrel plots evil,
and his speech is like a scorching fire.

28A perverse man stirs up dissension,
and a gossip separates close friends.

29A violent man entices his neighbor
and leads him down a path that is not good.

[a] 21 Or *words make a man persuasive* [b] 23 Or *and makes his lips persuasive*

[30]He who winks with his eye is plotting perversity;
he who purses his lips is bent on evil.

[31]Gray hair is a crown of splendor;
it is attained by a righteous life.

[32]Better a patient man than a warrior,
a man who controls his temper than one who takes a city.

[33]The lot is cast into the lap,
but its every decision is from the LORD.

17

Better a dry crust with peace and quiet
than a house full of feasting,[a] with strife.

[2]A wise servant will rule over a disgraceful son,
and will share the inheritance as one of the brothers.

[3]The crucible for silver and the furnace for gold,
but the LORD tests the heart.

[4]A wicked man listens to evil lips;
a liar pays attention to a malicious tongue.

[5]He who mocks the poor shows contempt for their Maker;
whoever gloats over disaster will not go unpunished.

[6]Children's children are a crown to the aged,
and parents are the pride of their children.

[7]Arrogant[b] lips are unsuited to a fool—
how much worse lying lips to a ruler!

[8]A bribe is a charm to the one who gives it;
wherever he turns, he succeeds.

[a] *1* Hebrew *sacrifices* [b] *7* Or *Eloquent*

[9]He who covers over an offense promotes love,
but whoever repeats the matter separates close friends.

[10]A rebuke impresses a man of discernment
more than a hundred lashes a fool.

[11]An evil man is bent only on rebellion;
a merciless official will be sent against him.

[12]Better to meet a bear robbed of her cubs
than a fool in his folly.

[13]If a man pays back evil for good,
evil will never leave his house.

[14]Starting a quarrel is like breaching a dam;
so drop the matter before a dispute breaks out.

[15]Acquitting the guilty and condemning the innocent—
the LORD detests them both.

[16]Of what use is money in the hand of a fool,
since he has no desire to get wisdom?

[17]A friend loves at all times,
and a brother is born for adversity.

[18]A man lacking in judgment strikes hands in pledge
and puts up security for his neighbor.

[19]He who loves a quarrel loves sin;
he who builds a high gate invites destruction.

[20]A man of perverse heart does not prosper;
he whose tongue is deceitful falls into trouble.

[21]To have a fool for a son brings grief;
there is no joy for the father of a fool.

[22]A cheerful heart is good medicine,
but a crushed spirit dries up the bones.

[23]A wicked man accepts a bribe in secret
to pervert the course of justice.

[24]A discerning man keeps wisdom in view,
but a fool's eyes wander to the ends of the
earth.

[25]A foolish son brings grief to his father
and bitterness to the one who bore him.

[26]It is not good to punish an innocent man,
or to flog officials for their integrity.

[27]A man of knowledge uses words with restraint,
and a man of understanding is even-tempered.

[28]Even a fool is thought wise if he keeps silent,
and discerning if he holds his tongue.

18 An unfriendly man pursues selfish ends;
he defies all sound judgment.

[2]A fool finds no pleasure in understanding,
but delights in airing his own opinions.

[3]When wickedness comes, so does contempt,
and with shame comes disgrace.

[4]The words of a man's mouth are deep waters,
but the fountain of wisdom is a bubbling
brook.

[5]It is not good to be partial to the wicked
or to deprive the innocent of justice.

[6]A fool's lips bring him strife,
and his mouth invites a beating.

[7]A fool's mouth is his undoing,
and his lips are a snare to his soul.

[8]The words of a gossip are like choice morsels;
they go down to a man's inmost parts.

[9]One who is slack in his work
is brother to one who destroys.

[10]The name of the LORD is a strong tower;
the righteous run to it and are safe.

[11]The wealth of the rich is their fortified city;
they imagine it an unscalable wall.

[12]Before his downfall a man's heart is proud,
but humility comes before honor.

[13]He who answers before listening—
that is his folly and his shame.

[14]A man's spirit sustains him in sickness,
but a crushed spirit who can bear?

[15]The heart of the discerning acquires knowledge;
the ears of the wise seek it out.

[16]A gift opens the way for the giver
and ushers him into the presence of the great.

[17]The first to present his case seems right,
till another comes forward and questions him.

[18]Casting the lot settles disputes
and keeps strong opponents apart.

[19]An offended brother is more unyielding than a fortified city,
and disputes are like the barred gates of a citadel.

[20]From the fruit of his mouth a man's stomach is filled;
with the harvest from his lips he is satisfied.

[21]The tongue has the power of life and death,
and those who love it will eat its fruit.

[22]He who finds a wife finds what is good
and receives favor from the LORD.

[23]A poor man pleads for mercy,
but a rich man answers harshly.

[24]A man of many companions may come to ruin,
but there is a friend who sticks closer than a brother.

19 Better a poor man whose walk is blameless
than a fool whose lips are perverse.

[2]It is not good to have zeal without knowledge,
nor to be hasty and miss the way.

[3]A man's own folly ruins his life,
yet his heart rages against the LORD.

[4]Wealth brings many friends,
but a poor man's friend deserts him.

[5]A false witness will not go unpunished,
and he who pours out lies will not go free.

[6]Many curry favor with a ruler,
and everyone is the friend of a man who gives gifts.

[7]A poor man is shunned by all his relatives—
how much more do his friends avoid him!
Though he pursues them with pleading,
they are nowhere to be found.[a]

[8]He who gets wisdom loves his own soul;
he who cherishes understanding prospers.

[a] 7 The meaning of the Hebrew sentence is uncertain.

[9]A false witness will not go unpunished,
and he who pours out lies will perish.

[10]It is not fitting for a fool to live in luxury—
how much worse for a slave to rule over princes!

[11]A man's wisdom gives him patience;
it is to his glory to overlook an offense.

[12]A king's rage is like the roar of a lion,
but his favor is like dew on the grass.

[13]A foolish son is his father's ruin,
and a quarrelsome wife is like a constant dripping.

[14]Houses and wealth are inherited from parents,
but a prudent wife is from the LORD.

[15]Laziness brings on deep sleep,
and the shiftless man goes hungry.

[16]He who obeys instructions guards his soul,
but he who is contemptuous of his ways will die.

[17]He who is kind to the poor lends to the LORD,
and he will reward him for what he has done.

[18]Discipline your son, for in that there is hope;
do not be a willing party to his death.

[19]A hot-tempered man must pay the penalty;
if you rescue him, you will have to do it again.

[20]Listen to advice and accept instruction,
and in the end you will be wise.

[21]Many are the plans in a man's heart,
but it is the LORD's purpose that prevails.

[22]What a man desires is unfailing love;[a]
better to be poor than a liar.

[23]The fear of the LORD leads to life:
Then one rests content, untouched by trouble.

[24]The sluggard buries his hand in the dish;
he will not even bring it back to his mouth!

[25]Flog a mocker, and the simple will learn prudence;
rebuke a discerning man, and he will gain knowledge.

[26]He who robs his father and drives out his mother
is a son who brings shame and disgrace.

[27]Stop listening to instruction, my son,
and you will stray from the words of knowledge.

[28]A corrupt witness mocks at justice,
and the mouth of the wicked gulps down evil.

[29]Penalties are prepared for mockers,
and beatings for the backs of fools.

20 Wine is a mocker and beer a brawler;
whoever is led astray by them is not wise.

[2]A king's wrath is like the roar of a lion;
he who angers him forfeits his life.

[3]It is to a man's honor to avoid strife,
but every fool is quick to quarrel.

[4]A sluggard does not plow in season;
so at harvest time he looks but finds nothing.

[a] 22 Or *A man's greed is his shame*

[5]The purposes of a man's heart are deep waters,
but a man of understanding draws them out.

[6]Many a man claims to have unfailing love,
but a faithful man who can find?

[7]The righteous man leads a blameless life;
blessed are his children after him.

[8]When a king sits on his throne to judge,
he winnows out all evil with his eyes.

[9]Who can say, "I have kept my heart pure;
I am clean and without sin"?

[10]Differing weights and differing measures—
the LORD detests them both.

[11]Even a child is known by his actions,
by whether his conduct is pure and right.

[12]Ears that hear and eyes that see—
the LORD has made them both.

[13]Do not love sleep or you will grow poor;
stay awake and you will have food to spare.

[14]"It's no good, it's no good!" says the buyer;
then off he goes and boasts about his
purchase.

[15]Gold there is, and rubies in abundance,
but lips that speak knowledge are a rare jewel.

[16]Take the garment of one who puts up security
for a stranger;
hold it in pledge if he does it for a wayward
woman.

[17]Food gained by fraud tastes sweet to a man,
but he ends up with a mouth full of gravel.

[18]Make plans by seeking advice;
if you wage war, obtain guidance.

[19]A gossip betrays a confidence;
so avoid a man who talks too much.

[20]If a man curses his father or mother,
his lamp will be snuffed out in pitch darkness.

[21]An inheritance quickly gained at the beginning
will not be blessed at the end.

[22]Do not say, "I'll pay you back for this wrong!"
Wait for the LORD, and he will deliver you.

[23]The LORD detests differing weights,
and dishonest scales do not please him.

[24]A man's steps are directed by the LORD;
how then can anyone understand his own way?

[25]It is a trap for a man to dedicate something rashly
and only later to consider his vows.

[26]A wise king winnows out the wicked;
he drives the threshing wheel over them.

[27]The lamp of the LORD searches the spirit of a man;[a]
it searches out his inmost being.

[28]Love and faithfulness keep a king safe;
through love his throne is made secure.

[29]The glory of young men is their strength,
gray hair the splendor of the old.

[30]Blows and wounds cleanse away evil,
and beatings purge the inmost being.

[a] 27 Or *The spirit of man is the LORD's lamp*

21 The king's heart is in the hand of the LORD;
he directs it like a watercourse wherever he pleases.

2All a man's ways seem right to him,
but the LORD weighs the heart.

3To do what is right and just
is more acceptable to the LORD than sacrifice.

4Haughty eyes and a proud heart,
the lamp of the wicked, are sin!

5The plans of the diligent lead to profit
as surely as haste leads to poverty.

6A fortune made by a lying tongue
is a fleeting vapor and a deadly snare.[a]

7The violence of the wicked will drag them away,
for they refuse to do what is right.

8The way of the guilty is devious,
but the conduct of the innocent is upright.

9Better to live on a corner of the roof
than share a house with a quarrelsome wife.

10The wicked man craves evil;
his neighbor gets no mercy from him.

11When a mocker is punished, the simple gain wisdom;
when a wise man is instructed, he gets knowledge.

12The Righteous One[b] takes note of the house of the wicked
and brings the wicked to ruin.

[a] 6 Some Hebrew manuscripts, Septuagint and Vulgate; most Hebrew manuscripts *vapor for those who seek death* [b] 12 Or *The righteous man*

[13]If a man shuts his ears to the cry of the poor,
he too will cry out and not be answered.

[14]A gift given in secret soothes anger,
and a bribe concealed in the cloak pacifies great wrath.

[15]When justice is done, it brings joy to the righteous
but terror to evildoers.

[16]A man who strays from the path of understanding
comes to rest in the company of the dead.

[17]He who loves pleasure will become poor;
whoever loves wine and oil will never be rich.

[18]The wicked become a ransom for the righteous,
and the unfaithful for the upright.

[19]Better to live in a desert
than with a quarrelsome and ill-tempered wife.

[20]In the house of the wise are stores of choice food and oil,
but a foolish man devours all he has.

[21]He who pursues righteousness and love
finds life, prosperity[a] and honor.

[22]A wise man attacks the city of the mighty
and pulls down the stronghold in which they trust.

[23]He who guards his mouth and his tongue
keeps himself from calamity.

[24]The proud and arrogant man—"Mocker" is his name;

[a] *21* Or *righteousness*

he behaves with overweaning pride.

[25]The sluggard's craving will be the death of him,
because his hands refuse to work.
[26]All day long he craves for more,
but the righteous give without sparing.

[27]The sacrifice of the wicked is detestable—
how much more so when brought with evil
intent!

[28]A false witness will perish,
and whoever listens to him will be destroyed
forever.[a]

[29]A wicked man puts up a bold front,
but an upright man gives thought to his ways.

[30]There is no wisdom, no insight, no plan
that can succeed against the LORD.

[31]The horse is made ready for the day of battle,
but victory rests with the LORD.

22 A good name is more desirable than great riches;
to be esteemed is better than silver or gold.

[2]Rich and poor have this in common:
The LORD is the Maker of them all.

[3]A prudent man sees danger and takes refuge,
but the simple keep going and suffer for it.

[4]Humility and the fear of the LORD
bring wealth and honor and life.

[5]In the paths of the wicked lie thorns and snares,
but he who guards his soul stays far from
them.

[a] 28 Or *but the words of an obedient man will live on*

[6]Train a child in the way he should go,
and when he is old he will not turn
from it.

[7]The rich rule over the poor,
and the borrower is servant to the lender.

[8]He who sows wickedness reaps trouble,
and the rod of his fury will be destroyed.

[9]A generous man will himself be blessed,
for he shares his food with the poor.

[10]Drive out the mocker, and out goes strife;
quarrels and insults are ended.

[11]He who loves a pure heart and whose speech is
gracious
will have the king for his friend.

[12]The eyes of the LORD keep watch over
knowledge,
but he frustrates the words of the
unfaithful.

[13]The sluggard says, "There is a lion outside!"
or, "I will be murdered in the streets!"

[14]The mouth of an adulteress is a deep pit;
he who is under the LORD's wrath will fall
into it.

[15]Folly is bound up in the heart of a child,
but the rod of discipline will drive it far from
him.

[16]He who oppresses the poor to increase his
wealth
and he who gives gifts to the rich—both come
to poverty.

Sayings of the Wise

[17]Pay attention and listen to the sayings of the wise;
apply your heart to what I teach,
[18]for it is pleasing when you keep them in your heart
and have all of them ready on your lips.
[19]So that your trust may be in the LORD,
I teach you today, even you.
[20]Have I not written thirty[a] sayings for you,
sayings of counsel and knowledge,
[21]teaching you true and reliable words,
so that you can give sound answers to him who sent you?

[22]Do not exploit the poor because they are poor
and do not crush the needy in court,
[23]for the LORD will take up their case
and will plunder those who plunder them.

[24]Do not make friends with a hot-tempered man,
do not associate with one easily angered,
[25]or you may learn his ways
and get yourself ensnared.

[26]Do not be a man who strikes hands in pledge
or puts up security for debts;
[27]if you lack the means to pay,
your very bed will be snatched from under you.

[28]Do not move an ancient boundary stone
set up by your forefathers.

[29]Do you see a man skilled in his work?
He will serve before kings;
he will not serve before obscure men.

[a] *20* Or *not formerly written;* or *not written excellent*

23 When you sit to dine with a ruler,
note well what[a] is before you,
[2]and put a knife to your throat
if you are given to gluttony.
[3]Do not crave his delicacies,
for that food is deceptive.

[4]Do not wear yourself out to get rich;
have the wisdom to show restraint.
[5]Cast but a glance at riches, and they are gone,
for they will surely sprout wings
and fly off to the sky like an eagle.

[6]Do not eat the food of a stingy man,
do not crave his delicacies;
[7]for he is the kind of man
who is always thinking about the cost.[b]
"Eat and drink," he says to you,
but his heart is not with you.
[8]You will vomit up the little you have eaten
and will have wasted your compliments.

[9]Do not speak to a fool,
for he will scorn the wisdom of your words.

[10]Do not move an ancient boundary stone
or encroach on the fields of the fatherless,
[11]for their Defender is strong;
he will take up their case against you.

[12]Apply your heart to instruction
and your ears to words of knowledge.

[13]Do not withhold discipline from a child;
if you punish him with the rod, he will not
die.
[14]Punish him with the rod

[a] 1 Or *who* [b] 7 Or *for as he thinks within himself, so he is;* or *for as he puts on a feast, so he is*

and save his soul from death.[a]

[15]My son, if your heart is wise,
then my heart will be glad;
[16]my inmost being will rejoice
when your lips speak what is right.

[17]Do not let your heart envy sinners,
but always be zealous for the fear of the LORD.
[18]There is surely a future hope for you,
and your hope will not be cut off.

[19]Listen, my son, and be wise,
and keep your heart on the right path.
[20]Do not join those who drink too much wine
or gorge themselves on meat,
[21]for drunkards and gluttons become poor,
and drowsiness clothes them in rags.

[22]Listen to your father, who gave you life,
and do not despise your mother when she is old.
[23]Buy the truth and do not sell it;
get wisdom, discipline and understanding.
[24]The father of a righteous man has great joy;
he who has a wise son delights in him.
[25]May your father and mother be glad;
may she who gave you birth rejoice!

[26]My son, give me your heart
and let your eyes keep to my ways,
[27]for a prostitute is a deep pit
and a wayward wife is a narrow well.
[28]Like a bandit she lies in wait,
and multiplies the unfaithful among men.

[29]Who has woe? Who has sorrow?
Who has strife? Who has complaints?

[a] *14* Hebrew *Sheol*

Who has needless bruises? Who has bloodshot eyes?
[30]Those who linger over wine,
who go to sample bowls of mixed wine.
[31]Do not gaze at wine when it is red,
when it sparkles in the cup,
when it goes down smoothly!
[32]In the end it bites like a snake
and poisons like a viper.
[33]Your eyes will see strange sights
and your mind imagine confusing things.
[34]You will be like one sleeping on the high seas,
lying on top of the rigging.
[35]"They hit me," you will say, "but I'm not hurt!
They beat me, but I don't feel it!
When will I wake up
so I can find another drink?"

24 Do not envy wicked men,
do not desire their company;
[2]for their hearts plot violence,
and their lips talk about making trouble.

[3]By wisdom a house is built,
and through understanding it is established;
[4]through knowledge its rooms are filled
with rare and beautiful treasures.

[5]A wise man has great power,
and a man of knowledge increases strength;
[6]for waging war you need guidance,
and for victory many advisers.

[7]Wisdom is too high for a fool;
in the assembly at the gate he has nothing to say.

[8]He who plots evil
will be known as a schemer.

[9]The schemes of folly are sin,
and men detest a mocker.

[10]If you falter in times of trouble,
how small is your strength!

[11]Rescue those being led away to death;
hold back those staggering toward slaughter.
[12]If you say, "But we knew nothing about this,"
does not he who weighs the heart perceive it?
Does not he who guards your life know it?
Will he not repay each person according to
what he has done?

[13]Eat honey, my son, for it is good;
honey from the comb is sweet to your taste.
[14]Know also that wisdom is sweet to your soul;
if you find it, there is a future hope for you,
and your hope will not be cut off.

[15]Do not lie in wait like an outlaw against a
righteous man's house,
do not raid his dwelling place;
[16]for though a righteous man falls seven times, he
rises again,
but the wicked are brought down by
calamity.

[17]Do not gloat when your enemy falls;
when he stumbles, do not let your heart
rejoice,
[18]or the LORD will see and disapprove
and turn his wrath away from him.

[19]Do not fret because of evildoers
or be envious of the wicked,
[20]for the evil man has no future hope,
and the lamp of the wicked will be snuffed
out.

[21]Fear the LORD and the king, my son,
and do not join with the rebellious,
[22]for those two will send sudden destruction upon them,
and who knows what calamities they can bring?

Further Sayings of the Wise

[23]These also are sayings of the wise:

To show partiality in judging is not good:
[24]Whoever says to the guilty, "You are innocent"—
peoples will curse him and nations denounce him.
[25]But it will go well with those who convict the guilty,
and rich blessing will come upon them.

[26]An honest answer
is like a kiss on the lips.

[27]Finish your outdoor work
and get your fields ready;
after that, build your house.

[28]Do not testify against your neighbor without cause,
or use your lips to deceive.
[29]Do not say, "I'll do to him as he has done to me;
I'll pay that man back for what he did."

[30]I went past the field of the sluggard,
past the vineyard of the man who lacks judgment;
[31]thorns had come up everywhere,
the ground was covered with weeds,
and the stone wall was in ruins.
[32]I applied my heart to what I observed
and learned a lesson from what I saw:

[33]A little sleep, a little slumber,
a little folding of the hands to rest—
[34]and poverty will come on you like a bandit
and scarcity like an armed man.[a]

More Proverbs of Solomon

25 These are more proverbs of Solomon, copied by the men of Hezekiah king of Judah:

[2]It is the glory of God to conceal a matter;
to search out a matter is the glory of kings.

[3]As the heavens are high and the earth is deep,
so the hearts of kings are unsearchable.

[4]Remove the dross from the silver,
and out comes material for[b] the silversmith;
[5]remove the wicked from the king's presence,
and his throne will be established through righteousness.

[6]Do not exalt yourself in the king's presence,
and do not claim a place among great men;
[7]it is better for him to say to you, "Come up here,"
than for him to humiliate you before a nobleman.

[8]What you have seen with your eyes
do not bring[c] hastily to court,
for what will you do in the end
if your neighbor puts you to shame?

[9]If you argue your case with a neighbor,
do not betray another man's confidence,
[10]or he who hears it may shame you
and you will never lose your bad reputation.

[a] 34 Or *like a vagrant / and scarcity like a beggar* [b] 4 Or *comes a vessel from*
[c] 8 Or *nobleman / on whom you had set your eyes. / [8] Do not go*

[11]A word aptly spoken
is like apples of gold in settings of silver.

[12]Like an earring of gold or an ornament of fine gold
is a wise man's rebuke to a listening ear.

[13]Like the coolness of snow at harvest time
is a trustworthy messenger to those who send him;
he refreshes the spirit of his masters.

[14]Like clouds and wind without rain
is a man who boasts of gifts he does not give.

[15]Through patience a ruler can be persuaded,
and a gentle tongue can break a bone.

[16]If you find honey, eat just enough—
too much of it, and you will vomit.
[17]Seldom set foot in your neighbor's house—
too much of you, and he will hate you.

[18]Like a club or a sword or a sharp arrow
is the man who gives false testimony against his neighbor.

[19]Like a bad tooth or a lame foot
is reliance on the unfaithful in times of trouble.

[20]Like one who takes away a garment on a cold day,
or like vinegar poured on soda,
is one who sings songs to a heavy heart.

[21]If your enemy is hungry, give him food to eat;
if he is thirsty, give him water to drink.
[22]In doing this, you will heap burning coals on his head,
and the LORD will reward you.

[23]As a north wind brings rain,
so a sly tongue brings angry looks.

[24]Better to live on a corner of the roof
than share a house with a quarrelsome wife.

[25]Like cold water to a weary soul
is good news from a distant land.

[26]Like a muddied spring or a polluted well
is a righteous man who gives way to the wicked.

[27]It is not good to eat too much honey,
nor is it honorable to seek one's own honor.

[28]Like a city whose walls are broken down
is a man who lacks self-control.

26

Like snow in summer or rain in harvest,
honor is not fitting for a fool.

[2]Like a fluttering sparrow or a darting swallow,
an undeserved curse does not come to rest.

[3]A whip for the horse, a halter for the donkey,
and a rod for the backs of fools!

[4]Do not answer a fool according to his folly,
or you will be like him yourself.

[5]Answer a fool according to his folly,
or he will be wise in his own eyes.

[6]Like cutting off one's feet or drinking violence
is the sending of a message by the hand of a fool.

[7]Like a lame man's legs that hang limp
is a proverb in the mouth of a fool.

[8]Like tying a stone in a sling
is the giving of honor to a fool.

[9]Like a thornbush in a drunkard's hand
is a proverb in the mouth of a fool.

[10]Like an archer who wounds at random
is he who hires a fool or any passer-by.

[11]As a dog returns to its vomit,
so a fool repeats his folly.

[12]Do you see a man wise in his own eyes?
There is more hope for a fool than for him.

[13]The sluggard says, "There is a lion in the road,
a fierce lion roaming the streets!"

[14]As a door turns on its hinges,
so a sluggard turns on his bed.

[15]The sluggard buries his hand in the dish;
he is too lazy to bring it back to his mouth.

[16]The sluggard is wiser in his own eyes
than seven men who answer discreetly.

[17]Like one who seizes a dog by the ears
is a passer-by who meddles in a quarrel not his own.

[18]Like a madman shooting
firebrands or deadly arrows
[19]is a man who deceives his neighbor
and says, "I was only joking!"

[20]Without wood a fire goes out;
without gossip a quarrel dies down.

[21]As charcoal to embers and as wood to fire,
so is a quarrelsome man for kindling strife.

[22]The words of a gossip are like choice morsels;
they go down to a man's inmost parts.

[23]Like a coating of glaze[a] over earthenware
are fervent lips with an evil heart.

[24]A malicious man disguises himself with his lips,
but in his heart he harbors deceit.
[25]Though his speech is charming, do not believe him,
for seven abominations fill his heart.
[26]His malice may be concealed by deception,
but his wickedness will be exposed in the assembly.

[27]If a man digs a pit, he will fall into it;
if a man rolls a stone, it will roll back on him.

[28]A lying tongue hates those it hurts,
and a flattering mouth works ruin.

27 Do not boast about tomorrow,
for you do not know what a day may bring forth.

[2]Let another praise you, and not your own mouth;
someone else, and not your own lips.

[3]Stone is heavy and sand a burden,
but provocation by a fool is heavier than both.

[4]Anger is cruel and fury overwhelming,
but who can stand before jealousy?

[5]Better is open rebuke
than hidden love.

[a] 23 With a different word division of the Hebrew; Masoretic text *of silver dross*

[6]The kisses of an enemy may be profuse,
but faithful are the wounds of a friend.

[7]He who is full loathes honey,
but to the hungry even what is bitter tastes sweet.

[8]Like a bird that strays from its nest
is a man who strays from his home.

[9]Perfume and incense bring joy to the heart,
and the pleasantness of one's friend springs from his earnest counsel.

[10]Do not forsake your friend and the friend of your father,
and do not go to your brother's house when disaster strikes you—
better a neighbor nearby than a brother far away.

[11]Be wise, my son, and bring joy to my heart;
then I can answer anyone who treats me with contempt.

[12]The prudent see danger and take refuge,
but the simple keep going and suffer for it.

[13]Take the garment of one who puts up security for a stranger;
hold it in pledge if he does it for a wayward woman.

[14]If a man loudly blesses his neighbor early in the morning,
it will be taken as a curse.

[15]A quarrelsome wife is like
a constant dripping on a rainy day;
[16]restraining her is like restraining the wind
or grasping oil with the hand.

[17]As iron sharpens iron,
so one man sharpens another.

[18]He who tends a fig tree will eat its fruit,
and he who looks after his master will be honored.

[19]As water reflects a face,
so a man's heart reflects the man.

[20]Death and Destruction[a] are never satisfied,
and neither are the eyes of man.

[21]The crucible for silver and the furnace for gold,
but man is tested by the praise he receives.

[22]Though you grind a fool in a mortar,
grinding him like grain with a pestle,
you will not remove his folly from him.

[23]Be sure you know the condition of your flocks,
give careful attention to your herds;
[24]for riches do not endure forever,
and a crown is not secure for all generations.
[25]When the hay is removed and new growth appears
and the grass from the hills is gathered in,
[26]the lambs will provide you with clothing,
and the goats with the price of a field.
[27]You will have plenty of goats' milk
to feed you and your family
and to nourish your servant girls.

28

The wicked man flees though no one pursues,
but the righteous are as bold as a lion.

[2]When a country is rebellious, it has many rulers,
but a man of understanding and knowledge maintains order.

[a] 20 Hebrew *Sheol and Abaddon*

[3]A ruler[a] who oppresses the poor
is like a driving rain that leaves no crops.

[4]Those who forsake the law praise the wicked,
but those who keep the law resist them.

[5]Evil men do not understand justice,
but those who seek the LORD understand it fully.

[6]Better a poor man whose walk is blameless
than a rich man whose ways are perverse.

[7]He who keeps the law is a discerning son,
but a companion of gluttons disgraces his father.

[8]He who increases his wealth by exorbitant interest
amasses it for another, who will be kind to the poor.

[9]If anyone turns a deaf ear to the law,
even his prayers are detestable.

[10]He who leads the upright along an evil path
will fall into his own trap,
but the blameless will receive a good inheritance.

[11]A rich man may be wise in his own eyes,
but a poor man who has discernment sees through him.

[12]When the righteous triumph, there is great elation;
but when the wicked rise to power, men go into hiding.

[a] 3 Or *A poor man*

[13]He who conceals his sins does not prosper,
but whoever confesses and renounces them finds mercy.

[14]Blessed is the man who always fears the LORD,
but he who hardens his heart falls into trouble.

[15]Like a roaring lion or a charging bear
is a wicked man ruling over a helpless people.

[16]A tyrannical ruler lacks judgment,
but he who hates ill-gotten gain will enjoy a long life.

[17]A man tormented by the guilt of murder
will be a fugitive till death;
let no one support him.

[18]He whose walk is blameless is kept safe,
but he whose ways are perverse will suddenly fall.

[19]He who works his land will have abundant food,
but the one who chases fantasies will have his fill of poverty.

[20]A faithful man will be richly blessed,
but one eager to get rich will not go unpunished.

[21]To show partiality is not good—
yet a man will do wrong for a piece of bread.

[22]A stingy man is eager to get rich
and is unaware that poverty awaits him.

[23]He who rebukes a man will in the end gain more favor
than he who has a flattering tongue.

[24]He who robs his father or mother
and says, "It's not wrong"—

he is partner to him who destroys.

25 A greedy man stirs up dissension,
but he who trusts in the LORD will prosper.

26 He who trusts in himself is a fool,
but he who walks in wisdom is kept safe.

27 He who gives to the poor will lack nothing,
but he who closes his eyes to them receives many curses.

28 When the wicked rise to power, people go into hiding;
but when the wicked perish, the righteous thrive.

29 A man who remains stiff-necked after many rebukes
will suddenly be destroyed—without remedy.

2 When the righteous thrive, the people rejoice;
when the wicked rule, the people groan.

3 A man who loves wisdom brings joy to his father,
but a companion of prostitutes squanders his wealth.

4 By justice a king gives a country stability,
but one who is greedy for bribes tears it down.

5 Whoever flatters his neighbor
is spreading a net for his feet.

6 An evil man is snared by his own sin,
but a righteous one can sing and be glad.

7 The righteous care about justice for the poor,
but the wicked have no such concern.

[8]Mockers stir up a city,
but wise men turn away anger.

[9]If a wise man goes to court with a fool,
the fool rages and scoffs, and there is no peace.

[10]Bloodthirsty men hate a man of integrity
and seek to kill the upright.

[11]A fool gives full vent to his anger,
but a wise man keeps himself under control.

[12]If a ruler listens to lies,
all his officials become wicked.

[13]The poor man and the oppressor have this in common:
The LORD gives sight to the eyes of both.

[14]If a king judges the poor with fairness,
his throne will always be secure.

[15]The rod of correction imparts wisdom,
but a child left to itself disgraces his mother.

[16]When the wicked thrive, so does sin,
but the righteous will see their downfall.

[17]Discipline your son, and he will give you peace;
he will bring delight to your soul.

[18]Where there is no revelation, the people cast off restraint;
but blessed is he who keeps the law.

[19]A servant cannot be corrected by mere words;
though he understands, he will not respond.

[20]Do you see a man who speaks in haste?
There is more hope for a fool than for him.

[21]If a man pampers his servant from youth,

he will bring grief[a] in the end.

[22]An angry man stirs up dissension,
and a hot-tempered one commits many sins.

[23]A man's pride brings him low,
but a man of lowly spirit gains honor.

[24]The accomplice of a thief is his own enemy;
he is put under oath and dare not testify.

[25]Fear of man will prove to be a snare,
but whoever trusts in the LORD is kept safe.

[26]Many seek an audience with a ruler,
but it is from the LORD that man gets justice.

[27]The righteous detest the dishonest;
the wicked detest the upright.

Sayings of Agur

30 The sayings of Agur son of Jakeh—an oracle:[b]

This man declared to Ithiel,
to Ithiel and to Ucal:[c]

[2]"I am the most ignorant of men;
I do not have a man's understanding.
[3]I have not learned wisdom,
nor have I knowledge of the Holy One.
[4]Who has gone up to heaven and come down?
Who has gathered up the wind in the hollow of his hands?
Who has wrapped up the waters in his cloak?
Who has established all the ends of the earth?
What is his name, and the name of his son?
Tell me if you know!

[a] *21* See Septuagint; the meaning of the Hebrew word is uncertain
[b] *1* Or *Jakeh of Massa* [c] *1* Or with a different division of the Hebrew words, *declared, "I am weary, O God, / I am weary, O God, and I am faint.*

[5]"Every word of God is flawless;
he is a shield to those who take refuge in him.
[6]Do not add to his words,
or he will rebuke you and prove you a liar.

[7]"Two things I ask of you, O LORD;
do not refuse me before I die:
[8]Keep falsehood and lies far from me;
give me neither poverty nor riches,
but give me only my daily bread.
[9]Otherwise, I may have too much and disown
you
and say, 'Who is the LORD?'
Or I may become poor and steal,
and so dishonor the name of my God.

[10]"Do not slander a servant to his master,
or he will curse you, and you will pay for it.

[11]"There are those who curse their fathers
and do not bless their mothers;
[12]those who are pure in their own eyes
and yet are not cleansed of their filth;
[13]those whose eyes are ever so haughty,
whose glances are so disdainful;
[14]those whose teeth are swords
and whose jaws are set with knives
to devour the poor from the earth,
the needy from among mankind.

[15]"The leech has two daughters.
'Give! Give!' they cry.

"There are three things that are never satisfied,
four that never say, 'Enough!':

[16]the grave,[a] the barren womb,
land, which is never satisfied with water,
and fire, which never says, 'Enough!'

[17]"The eye that mocks a father,
that scorns obedience to a mother,
will be pecked out by the ravens of the valley,
will be eaten by the vultures.

[18]"There are three things that are too amazing for me,
four that I do not understand:
[19]the way of an eagle in the sky,
the way of a snake on a rock,
the way of a ship on the high seas,
and the way of a man with a maiden.

[20]"This is the way of an adulteress:
She eats and wipes her mouth
and says, 'I've done nothing wrong.'

[21]"Under three things the earth trembles,
under four it cannot bear up:
[22]a servant who becomes king,
a fool who is full of food,
[23]an unloved woman who is married,
and a maidservant who displaces her mistress.

[24]"Four things on earth are small,
yet they are extremely wise:
[25]Ants are creatures of little strength,
yet they store up their food in the summer;
[26]conies are creatures of little power,
yet they make their home in the crags;
[27]locusts have no king,

[a] *16* Hebrew *Sheol*

yet they advance together in ranks;
[28]a lizard can be caught with the hand,
yet it is found in kings' palaces.

[29]"There are three things that are stately in their stride,
four that move with stately bearing;
[30]a lion, mighty among beasts,
who retreats before nothing;
[31]a strutting rooster, a he-goat,
and a king with his army around him.[a]

[32]"If you have played the fool and exalted yourself,
or if you have planned evil,
clap your hand over your mouth!
[33]For as churning the milk produces butter,
and as twisting the nose produces blood,
so stirring up anger produces strife."

Sayings of King Lemuel

31 The sayings of King Lemuel—an oracle[b] his mother taught him:

[2]"O my son, O son of my womb,
O son of my vows,[c]
[3]do not spend your strength on women,
your vigor on those who ruin kings.

[4]"It is not for kings, O Lemuel—
not for kings to drink wine,
not for rulers to crave beer,
[5]lest they drink and forget what the law decrees,
and deprive all the oppressed of their rights.
[6]Give beer to those who are perishing,
wine to those who are in anguish;

[a] 31 Or *king secure against revolt* [b] 1 Or *of Lemuel king of Massa*
[c] 2 Or *womb, / the answer to my prayers*

[7]let them drink and forget their poverty
and remember their misery no more.

[8]"Speak up for those who cannot speak for
themselves,
for the rights of all who are destitute.
[9]Speak up and judge fairly;
defend the rights of the poor and needy."

Epilogue: The Wife of Noble Character

[10][a]A wife of noble character who can find?
She is worth far more than rubies.
[11]Her husband has full confidence in her
and lacks nothing of value.
[12]She brings him good, not harm,
all the days of her life.
[13]She selects wool and flax
and works with eager hands.
[14]She is like the merchant ships,
bringing her food from afar.
[15]She gets up while it is still dark;
she provides food for her family
and portions for her servant girls.
[16]She considers a field and buys it;
out of her earnings she plants a vineyard.
[17]She sets about her work vigorously;
her arms are strong for her tasks.
[18]She sees that her trading is profitable,
and her lamp does not go out at night.
[19]In her hand she holds the distaff
and grasps the spindle with her fingers.
[20]She opens her arms to the poor
and extends her hands to the needy.

[a] *10* Verses 10-31 are an acrostic, each verse beginning with a consecutive letter of the Hebrew alphabet.

[21]When it snows, she has no fear for her
household;
for all of them are clothed in scarlet.
[22]She makes coverings for her bed;
she is clothed in fine linen and purple.
[23]Her husband is respected at the city gate,
where he takes his seat among the elders of
the land.
[24]She makes linen garments and sells them,
and supplies the merchants with sashes.
[25]She is clothed with strength and dignity;
she can laugh at the days to come.
[26]She speaks with wisdom,
and faithful instruction is on her tongue.
[27]She watches over the affairs of her household
and does not eat the bread of idleness.
[28]Her children arise and call her blessed;
her husband also, and he praises her:
[29]"Many women do noble things,
but you surpass them all."
[30]Charm is deceptive, and beauty is fleeting;
but a woman who fears the LORD is to be
praised.
[31]Give her the reward she has earned,
and let her works bring her praise at the city
gate.

Ecclesiastes

Ecclesiastes

Everything Is Meaningless

1 The words of the Teacher,[a] son of David, king in Jerusalem:

[2]"Meaningless! Meaningless!"
says the Teacher.[a]
"Utterly meaningless!
Everything is meaningless."

[3]What does man gain from all his labor
at which he toils under the sun?
[4]Generations come and generations go,
but the earth remains forever.
[5]The sun rises and the sun sets,
and hurries back to where it rises.
[6]The wind blows to the south
and turns to the north;
round and round it goes,
ever returning on its course.
[7]All streams flow into the sea,
yet the sea is never full.
To the place the streams come from,
there they return again.
[8]All things are wearisome,
more than one can say.
The eye never has enough of seeing,
or the ear its fill of hearing.

[a] *1, 2* Or *the leader of the assembly*

[9]What has been will be again,
what has been done will be done again;
there is nothing new under the sun.
[10]Is there anything of which one can say,
"Look! This is something new"?
It was here already, long ago;
it was here before our time.
[11]There is no remembrance of men of old,
and even those who are yet to come
will not be remembered
by those who follow.

Wisdom Is Meaningless

[12]I, the Teacher,[a] was king over Israel in Jerusalem. [13]I devoted myself to study and to explore by wisdom all that is done under heaven. What a heavy burden God has laid on men! [14]I have seen all the things that are done under the sun; all of them are meaningless, a chasing after the wind.

[15]What is twisted cannot be straightened;
what is lacking cannot be counted.

[16]I thought to myself, "Look, I have grown and increased in wisdom more than anyone who has ruled over Jerusalem before me; I have experienced much of wisdom and knowledge." [17]Then I applied myself to the understanding of wisdom, and also of madness and folly, but I learned that this, too, is a chasing after the wind.

[18]For with much wisdom comes much sorrow;
the more knowledge, the more grief.

Pleasures Are Meaningless

2 I thought in my heart, "Come now, I will test you with pleasure to find out what is good." But that also proved to be meaningless. [2]"Laughter," I said, "is foolish. And what does pleasure accomplish?" [3]I tried cheering myself with

[a] *12* Or *the leader of the assembly*

wine, and embracing folly—my mind still guiding me with wisdom. I wanted to see what was worthwhile for men to do under heaven during the few days of their lives.

4I undertook great projects: I built houses for myself and planted vineyards. 5I made gardens and parks and planted all kinds of fruit trees in them. 6I made reservoirs to water groves of flourishing trees. 7I bought male and female slaves and had other slaves who were born in my house. I also owned more herds and flocks than anyone in Jerusalem before me. 8I amassed silver and gold for myself, and the treasure of kings and provinces. I acquired men and women singers, and a harem[a] as well—the delights of the heart of man. 9I became greater by far than anyone in Jerusalem before me. In all this my wisdom stayed with me.

10I denied myself nothing my eyes desired;
I refused my heart no pleasure.
My heart took delight in all my work,
and this was the reward for all my labor.
11Yet when I surveyed all that my hands had done
and what I had toiled to achieve,
everything was meaningless, a chasing after the wind;
nothing was gained under the sun.

Wisdom and Folly Are Meaningless

12Then I turned my thoughts to consider wisdom,
and also madness and folly.
What more can the king's successor do
than what has already been done?
13I saw that wisdom is better than folly,
just as light is better than darkness.
14The wise man has eyes in his head,
while the fool walks in the darkness;
but I came to realize
that the same fate overtakes them both.

[a] *8* The meaning of the Hebrew phrase is uncertain.

[15]Then I thought in my heart,

"The fate of the fool will overtake me also.
What then do I gain by being wise?"
I said in my heart,
"This too is meaningless."
[16]For the wise man, like the fool, will not be long remembered;
in days to come both will be forgotten.
Like the fool, the wise man too must die!

Toil Is Meaningless

[17]So I hated life, because the work that is done under the sun was grievous to me. All of it is meaningless, a chasing after the wind. [18]I hated all the things I had toiled for under the sun, because I must leave them to the one who comes after me. [19]And who knows whether he will be a wise man or a fool? Yet he will have control over all the work into which I have poured my effort and skill under the sun. This too is meaningless. [20]So my heart began to despair over all my toilsome labor under the sun. [21]For a man may do his work with wisdom, knowledge and skill, and then he must leave all he owns to someone who has not worked for it. This too is meaningless and a great misfortune. [22]What does a man get for all the toil and anxious striving with which he labors under the sun? [23]All his days his work is pain and grief; even at night his mind does not rest. This too is meaningless.

[24]A man can do nothing better than to eat and drink and find satisfaction in his work. This too, I see, is from the hand of God, [25]for without him, who can eat or find enjoyment? [26]To the man who pleases him, God gives wisdom, knowledge and happiness, but to the sinner he gives the task of gathering and storing up wealth to hand it over to the one who pleases God. This too is meaningless, a chasing after the wind.

A Time for Everything

3 There is a time for everything,
and a season for every activity under heaven:

[2] a time to be born and a time to die,
a time to plant and a time to uproot,
[3] a time to kill and a time to heal,
a time to tear down and a time to build,
[4] a time to weep and a time to laugh,
a time to mourn and a time to dance,
[5] a time to scatter stones and a time to gather them,
a time to embrace and a time to refrain,
[6] a time to search and a time to give up,
a time to keep and a time to throw away,
[7] a time to tear and a time to mend,
a time to be silent and a time to speak,
[8] a time to love and a time to hate,
a time for war and a time for peace.

[9]What does the worker gain from his toil? [10]I have seen the burden God has laid on men. [11]He has made everything beautiful in its time. He has also set eternity in the hearts of men; yet they cannot fathom what God has done from beginning to end. [12]I know that there is nothing better for men than to be happy and do good while they live. [13]That every man may eat and drink, and find satisfaction in all his toil—this is the gift of God. [14]I know that everything God does will endure forever; nothing can be added to it and nothing taken from it. God does it, so men will revere him.

[15]Whatever is has already been,
and what will be has been before;
and God will call the past to account.[a]

[16]And I saw something else under the sun:

[a] *15* Or *God calls back the past*

In the place of judgment—wickedness was there,
  in the place of justice—wickedness was there.

17I thought in my heart,

"God will bring to judgment
  both the righteous and the wicked,
for there will be a time for every activity,
  a time for every deed."

18I also thought, "As for men, God tests them so that they may see that they are like the animals. 19Man's fate is like that of the animals; the same fate awaits them both: As one dies, so dies the other. All have the same breath[a]; man has no advantage over the animal. Everything is meaningless. 20All go to the same place; all come from dust, and to dust all return. 21Who knows if the spirit of man rises upward and if the spirit of the animal goes down into the earth?"[b]

22So I saw that there is nothing better for a man than to enjoy his work, because that is his lot. For who can bring him to see what will happen after him?

Oppression, Toil, Friendlessness

4 Again I looked and saw all the oppression that was taking place under the sun:

I saw the tears of the oppressed—
  and they have no comforter;
power was on the side of their oppressors—
  and they have no comforter.
2And I declared that the dead,
  who had already died,
are happier than the living,
  who are still alive.
3But better than both
  is he who has not yet been,

[a] *19* Or *spirit* [b] *21* Or *Who knows the spirit of man, which rises upward, or the spirit of the animal, which goes down into the earth?"*

who has not seen the evil
  that is done under the sun.

[4]And I saw that all labor and all achievement spring from man's envy of his neighbor. This too is meaningless, a chasing after the wind.

[5]The fool folds his hands
  and ruins himself.
[6]Better one handful with tranquillity
  than two handfuls with toil
  and chasing after the wind.

[7]Again I saw something meaningless under the sun:

[8]There was a man all alone;
  he had neither son nor brother.
There was no end to his toil,
  yet his eyes were not content with his wealth.
"For whom am I toiling," he asked,
  "and why am I depriving myself of
    enjoyment?"
This too is meaningless—
  a miserable business!

[9]Two are better than one,
  because they have a good return for their
    work:
[10]If one falls down,
  his friend can help him up.
But pity the man who falls
  and has no one to help him up!
[11]Also, if two lie down together, they will keep
    warm;
  but how can one keep warm alone?
[12]Though one may be overpowered,
  two can defend themselves.
A cord of three strands is not quickly broken.

Advancement Is Meaningless

[13]Better a poor but wise youth than an old but foolish king who no longer knows how to take warning. [14]The youth may have come from prison to the kingship, or he may have been born in poverty within his kingdom. [15]I saw that all who lived and walked under the sun followed the youth, the king's successor. [16]There was no end to all the people who were before them. But those who came later were not pleased with the successor. This too is meaningless, a chasing after the wind.

Stand in Awe of God

5 Guard your steps when you go to the house of God. Go near to listen rather than to offer the sacrifice of fools, who do not know that they do wrong.

[2]Do not be quick with your mouth,
do not be hasty in your heart
to utter anything before God.
God is in heaven
and you are on earth,
so let your words be few.
[3]As a dream comes when there are many cares,
so the speech of a fool when there are many words.

[4]When you make a vow to God, do not delay in fulfilling it. He has no pleasure in fools; fulfill your vow. [5]It is better not to vow than to make a vow and not fulfill it. [6]Do not let your mouth lead you into sin. And do not protest to the ⌊temple⌋ messenger, "My vow was a mistake." Why should God be angry at what you say and destroy the work of your hands? [7]Much dreaming and many words are meaningless. Therefore stand in awe of God.

Riches Are Meaningless

[8]If you see the poor oppressed in a district, and justice and rights denied, do not be surprised at such things; for one official is eyed by a higher one, and over them both are others higher still. [9]The increase from the land is taken by all; the king himself profits from the fields.

[10]Whoever loves money never has money enough;
whoever loves wealth is never satisfied with
his income.
This too is meaningless.

[11]As goods increase,
so do those who consume them.
And what benefit are they to the owner
except to feast his eyes on them?

[12]The sleep of a laborer is sweet,
whether he eats little or much,
but the abundance of a rich man
permits him no sleep.

[13]I have seen a grievous evil under the sun:

wealth hoarded to the harm of its owner,
[14] or wealth lost through some misfortune,
so that when he has a son
there is nothing left for him.
[15]Naked a man comes from his mother's womb,
and as he comes, so he departs.
He takes nothing from his labor
that he can carry in his hand.

[16]This too is a grievous evil:

As a man comes, so he departs,
and what does he gain,
since he toils for the wind?
[17]All his days he eats in darkness,
with great frustration, affliction and anger.

[18]Then I realized that it is good and proper for a man to eat and drink, and to find satisfaction in his toilsome labor under the sun during the few days of life God has given him—for this is his lot. [19]Moreover, when God gives any man wealth and possessions, and enables him to enjoy them, to accept his lot and be happy in his work—this is a gift of God. [20]He seldom reflects on the days of his life, because God keeps him occupied with gladness of heart.

6 I have seen another evil under the sun, and it weighs heavily on men: [2]God gives a man wealth, possessions and honor, so that he lacks nothing his heart desires, but God does not enable him to enjoy them, and a stranger enjoys them instead. This is meaningless, a grievous evil.

[3]A man may have a hundred children and live many years; yet no matter how long he lives, if he cannot enjoy his prosperity and does not receive proper burial, I say that a stillborn child is better off than he. [4]It comes without meaning, it departs in darkness, and in darkness its name is shrouded. [5]Though it never saw the sun or knew anything, it has more rest than does that man— [6]even if he lives a thousand years twice over but fails to enjoy his prosperity. Do not all go to the same place?

[7]All man's efforts are for his mouth,
yet his appetite is never satisfied.
[8]What advantage has a wise man
over a fool?
What does a poor man gain
by knowing how to conduct himself before
others?
[9]Better what the eye sees
than the roving of the appetite.
This too is meaningless,
a chasing after the wind.

[10]Whatever exists has already been named,
and what man is has been known;
no man can contend

with one who is stronger than he.
[11]The more the words,
the less the meaning;
and how does that profit anyone?

[12]For who knows what is good for a man in life, during the few and meaningless days he passes through like a shadow? Who can tell him what will happen under the sun after he is gone?

Wisdom

7 A good name is better than fine perfume,
and the day of death better than the day of birth.
[2]It is better to go to a house of mourning
than to go to a house of feasting,
for death is the destiny of every man;
the living should take this to heart.
[3]Sorrow is better than laughter,
because a sad face is good for the heart.
[4]The heart of the wise is in the house of mourning,
but the heart of fools is in the house of pleasure.
[5]It is better to heed a wise man's rebuke
than to listen to the song of fools.
[6]Like the crackling of thorns under the pot,
so is the laughter of fools.
This too is meaningless.

[7]Extortion turns a wise man into a fool,
and a bribe corrupts the heart.

[8]The end of a matter is better than its beginning,
and patience is better than pride.
[9]Do not be quickly provoked in your spirit,
for anger resides in the lap of fools.

[10]Do not say, "Why were the old days better than
these?"
For it is not wise to ask such questions.

[11]Wisdom, like an inheritance, is a good thing
and benefits those who see the sun.
[12]Wisdom is a shelter
as money is a shelter,
but the advantage of knowledge is this:
that wisdom preserves the life of its possessor.

[13]Consider what God has done:

Who can straighten
what he has made crooked?
[14]When times are good, be happy;
but when times are bad, consider:
God has made the one
as well as the other.
Therefore, a man cannot discover
anything about his future.

[15]In this meaningless life of mine I have seen both of these:

A righteous man perishing in his righteousness,
and a wicked man living long in his
wickedness.
[16]Do not be overrighteous,
neither be overwise—
why destroy yourself?
[17]Do not be overwicked,
and do not be a fool—
why die before your time?
[18]It is good to grasp the one
and not let go of the other.
The man who fears God will avoid all
⌊extremes⌋.[a]

[a] *18* Or *will follow them both*

[19]Wisdom makes one wise man more powerful
than ten rulers in a city.

[20]There is not a righteous man on earth
who does what is right and never sins.

[21]Do not pay attention to every word people say,
or you may hear your servant cursing you—
[22]for you know in your heart
that many times you yourself have cursed
others.

[23]All this I tested by wisdom and I said,

"I am determined to be wise"—
but this was beyond me.
[24]Whatever wisdom may be,
it is far off and most profound—
who can discover it?
[25]So I turned my mind to understand,
to investigate and to search out wisdom and
the scheme of things
and to understand the stupidity of wickedness
and the madness of folly.

[26]I find more bitter than death
the woman who is a snare,
whose heart is a trap,
and whose hands are chains.
The man who pleases God will escape her,
but the sinner she will ensnare.

[27]"Look," says the Teacher,[a] "this is what I have discovered:

Adding one thing to another to discover the
scheme of things—
[28] while I was still searching
but not finding—

[a] 27 Or *the leader of the assembly*

I found one ⌞upright⌟ man among a thousand,
but not one ⌞upright⌟ woman among them all.
[29]This only have I found:
God made mankind upright,
but men have gone in search of many schemes."

8 Who is like the wise man?
Who knows the explanation of things?
Wisdom brightens a man's face
and changes its hard appearance.

Obey the King

[2]Obey the king's command, I say, because you took an oath before God. [3]Do not be in a hurry to leave the king's presence. Do not stand up for a bad cause, for he will do whatever he pleases. [4]Since a king's word is supreme, who can say to him, "What are you doing?"

[5]Whoever obeys his command will come to no harm,
and the wise heart will know the proper time and procedure.
[6]For there is a proper time and procedure for every matter,
though a man's misery weighs heavily upon him.

[7]Since no man knows the future,
who can tell him what is to come?
[8]No man has power over the wind to contain it[a];
so no one has power over the day of his death.
As no one is discharged in time of war,
so wickedness will not release those who practice it.

[9]All this I saw, as I applied my mind to everything done

[a] 8 Or *over his spirit to retain it*

under the sun. There is a time when a man lords it over others to his own[a] hurt. [10]Then too, I saw the wicked buried—those who used to come and go from the holy place and receive praise[b] in the city where they did this. This too is meaningless.

[11]When the sentence for a crime is not quickly carried out, the hearts of the people are filled with schemes to do wrong. [12]Although a wicked man commits a hundred crimes and still lives a long time, I know that it will go better with God-fearing men, who are reverent before God. [13]Yet because the wicked do not fear God, it will not go well with them, and their days will not lengthen like a shadow.

[14]There is something else meaningless that occurs on earth: righteous men who get what the wicked deserve, and wicked men who get what the righteous deserve. This too, I say, is meaningless. [15]So I commend the enjoyment of life, because nothing is better for a man under the sun than to eat and drink and be glad. Then joy will accompany him in his work all the days of the life God has given him under the sun.

[16]When I applied my mind to know wisdom and to observe man's labor on earth—his eyes not seeing sleep day or night— [17]then I saw all that God has done. No one can comprehend what goes on under the sun. Despite all his efforts to search it out, man cannot discover its meaning. Even if a wise man claims he knows, he cannot really comprehend it.

A Common Destiny for All

9 So I reflected on all this and concluded that the righteous and the wise and what they do are in God's hands, but no man knows whether love or hate awaits him. [2]All share a common destiny—the righteous and the wicked, the good and the bad,[c] the clean and the unclean, those who offer sacrifices and those who do not.

[a] 9 Or *to their* [b] 10 Some Hebrew manuscripts, Septuagint and Aquila; other Hebrew manuscripts *they are forgotten* [c] 2 Septuagint, Vulgate and Syriac; Hebrew does not have *and the bad*

As it is with the good man,
so with the sinner;
as it is with those who take oaths,
so with those who are afraid to take them.

[3]This is the evil in everything that happens under the sun: The same destiny overtakes all. The hearts of men, moreover, are full of evil and there is madness in their hearts while they live, and afterwards they join the dead. [4]Anyone who is among the living has hope[a]—even a live dog is better off than a dead lion!

[5]For the living know that they will die,
but the dead know nothing;
they have no further reward,
and even the memory of them is forgotten.
[6]Their love, their hate
and their jealousy have long since vanished;
never again will they have a part
in anything that happens under the sun.

[7]Go, eat your food with gladness,
and drink your wine with a joyful heart,
for it is now that God favors what you do.
[8]Always be clothed in white,
and always anoint your head with oil.

[9]Enjoy life with your wife, whom you love, all the days of this meaningless life that God has given you under the sun—all your meaningless days. For this is your lot in life and in your toilsome labor under the sun. [10]Whatever your hand finds to do, do it with all your might, for in the grave,[b] where you are going, there is neither working nor planning nor knowledge nor wisdom.

[11]I have seen something else under the sun:

The race is not to the swift

[a] *4* Ancient versions and many Hebrew manuscripts; other Hebrew manuscripts *What then is to be chosen? With all who live, there is hope* [b] *10* Hebrew *Sheol*

or the battle to the strong,
nor does food come to the wise
or wealth to the brilliant
or favor to the learned;
but time and chance happen to them all.

[12]Moreover, no man knows when his hour will come:

As fish are caught in a cruel net,
or birds are taken in a snare,
so men are trapped by evil times
that fall unexpectedly upon them.

Wisdom Better Than Folly

[13]I also saw under the sun this example of wisdom that greatly impressed me: [14]There was once a small city with only a few people in it. And a powerful king came against it, surrounded it and built huge siegeworks against it. [15]Now there lived in that city a man poor but wise, and he saved the city by his wisdom. But nobody remembered that poor man. [16]So I said, "Wisdom is better than strength." But the poor man's wisdom was despised, and his words were not heeded.

[17]The quiet words of the wise are more to be heeded
than the shouts of a ruler of fools.
[18]Wisdom is better than weapons of war,
but one sinner destroys much good.

10 As dead flies give perfume a bad smell,
so a little folly outweighs wisdom and honor.
[2]The heart of the wise inclines to the right,
but the heart of the fool to the left.
[3]Even as he walks along the road,
the fool lacks sense
and shows everyone how stupid he is.
[4]If a ruler's anger rises against you,
do not leave your post;

calmness can lay great errors to rest.

[5]There is an evil I have seen under the sun,
the sort of error that arises from a ruler:
[6]Fools are put in many high positions,
while the rich occupy the low ones.
[7]I have seen slaves on horseback,
while princes go on foot like slaves.

[8]Whoever digs a pit may fall into it;
whoever breaks through a wall may be bitten by a snake.
[9]Whoever quarries stones may be injured by them;
whoever splits logs may be endangered by them.

[10]If the axe is dull
and its edge unsharpened,
more strength is needed
but skill will bring success.

[11]If a snake bites before it is charmed,
there is no profit for the charmer.

[12]Words from a wise man's mouth are gracious,
but a fool is consumed by his own lips.
[13]At the beginning his words are folly;
at the end they are wicked madness—
[14] and the fool multiplies words.

No one knows what is coming;
who can tell him what will happen after him?

[15]A fool's work wearies him;
he does not know the way to town.

[16]Woe to you, O land, whose king was a servant,[a]
and whose princes feast in the morning.

[a] *16* Or *king is a child*

[17]Blessed are you, O land, whose king is of noble birth,
whose princes eat at a proper time—
for strength and not for drunkenness.

[18]If a man is lazy, the rafters sag;
if his hands are idle, the house leaks.

[19]A feast is made for laughter,
and wine makes life merry,
but money is the answer for everything.

[20]Do not revile the king even in your thoughts,
nor curse the rich in your bedroom,
because a bird of the air may carry your words,
and a bird on the wing may report what you say.

Bread Upon the Waters

11 Cast your bread upon the waters,
for after many days you will find it again.
[2]Give portions to seven, yes to eight,
for you do not know what disaster may come upon the land.

[3]If clouds are full of water,
they pour rain upon the earth.
Whether a tree falls to the south or to the north,
in the place where it falls, there will it lie.
[4]Whoever watches the wind will not plant;
whoever looks at the clouds will not reap.

[5]As you do not know the path of the wind,
or how the body is formed in a mother's womb,
so you cannot understand the work of God,
the Maker of all things.

[6]Sow your seed in the morning,
and at evening let not your hands be idle,
for you do not know which will succeed,
whether this or that,
or whether both will do equally well.

Remember Your Creator While Young

[7]Light is sweet,
and it pleases the eyes to see the sun.
[8]However many years a man may live,
let him enjoy them all.
But let him remember the days of darkness,
for they will be many.
Everything to come is meaningless.

[9]Be happy, young man, while you are young,
and let your heart give you joy in the days of your youth.
Follow the ways of your heart
and whatever your eyes see,
but know that for all these things
God will bring you to judgment.
[10]So then, banish anxiety from your heart
and cast off the troubles of your body,
for youth and vigor are meaningless.

12 Remember your Creator
in the days of your youth,
before the days of trouble come,
and the years approach when you will say,
"I find no pleasure in them"—
[2]before the sun and the light
and the moon and the stars grow dark,
and the clouds return after the rain;
[3]when the keepers of the house tremble,
and the strong men stoop,
when the grinders cease because they are few,

and those looking through the windows grow
dim;
[4]when the doors to the street are closed
and the sound of grinding fades;
when men rise up at the sound of birds,
but all their songs grow faint;
[5]when men are afraid of heights
and of dangers in the streets;
when the almond tree blossoms,
the grasshopper drags himself along,
and desire no longer is stirred.
Then man goes to his eternal home
and mourners go about the streets.

[6]Remember him—before the silver cord is
severed,[a]
or the golden bowl is broken;
before the pitcher is shattered at the spring,
or the wheel broken at the well,
[7]and the dust returns to the ground it came from,
and the spirit returns to God who gave it.

[8]"Meaningless! Meaningless!" says the Teacher.[b]
"Everything is meaningless!"

The Conclusion of the Matter

[9]Not only was the Teacher[b] wise, but also he imparted knowledge to the people. He pondered and searched out and set in order many proverbs. [10]The Teacher[b] searched to find just the right words, and what he wrote was upright and true.

[11]The words of the wise are like goads, their collected sayings like firmly embedded nails—given by one Shepherd. [12]Be warned, my son, of anything in addition to them.

[a] *6* Septuagint, Vulgate and Syriac; Hebrew *is removed* [b] *8, 9, 10* Or *the leader of the assembly*

Of making many books there is no end, and much study wearies the body.

[13]Now all has been heard;
here is the conclusion of the matter:
Fear God and keep his commandments
for this is the whole duty of man.
[14]For God will bring every deed into judgment,
including every hidden thing,
whether it is good or evil.